IMBRICATION

POEMS

Louis Sinclair

Copyright © 2016, Louis Sinclair

December, 2016 Edition
Times New Roman Typeface

imbrication.ls@gmail.com

Acknowledgements: Some of these poems (some in earlier versions) appeared in, *Southern Poetry Review, Maine Times, Innerspring, Omens, Portland Sunday Telegram, Ubris, Off the Coast, Kennebec: A Portfolio of Maine Writing, Onion River Review*

"The Deer," appeared in, *Prize Poems 1970,* published by, The Maine State Commission on the Arts and Humanities

Cover Image: *Imbrication #29,* by, Louis Sinclair — edition of ten prints, archival inkjet on 100% cotton paper, from the original collage

*For Eoin
and my family*

Table of Contents

Part I

Cape Alava, Olympic Peninsula   9

Where is the Magic?   12

Apartment Dweller   13

Migration   15

Flesh or Wood   16

Medicine Man   18

Something Magnificent   20

First Snow   23

Almost Lost in Time   25

Juju   27

Parallel Motion   29

Part II

Understanding, Fifty Miles Northwest of Fairbanks   31

When Turtles Called My Name   34

Last Night's Dream   36

Monday Night Barking   39

March Blizzard, Maine   40

The Deer   41

Mice in My Mind   43

Columbus Day   44

Alaska Wilderness   46

Steave and The Rambler   47

Part III

Civilization   50

Guatemala City - Belfast, N.I.   52

After Nicaragua   54

Red   56

Cherry Blossoms   57

The Mailboat   58

House on Inis Oírr   60

The Eve of Saint Brigid's Feast   62

Glencree Night   64

Dear Ants   66

Part IV

Porn Poem for Emily 68

Refugees on TV 70

Desert Museum Docent 72

The Prize 74

Translating a Dream of Death 76

Red, Spiral-Bound Notebook 78

Paradise 80

To Lee, Ki Bok 82

My Last Walk 83

Together 85

Part V

The Worms of Walden 87

IMBRICATION

Part I

A bit of fragrance always clings to the hand that dispenses roses
-Chinese proverb

Cape Alava, Olympic Peninsula

Walking over sand, surrounded by spitting
hiss of clams; bullwhip kelp tumbled
like balls of brown snakes in foamy surf;
boulders girded by lime seaweeds.

Three, fat, grunting seals, languished
on a granite slab; an eagle plunged
down into the sea, through salted mist,
tide slowly sucking everything out to sea.

"O to be a seal and drape my body
over a rock . . ." you said, spreading
your arms, to offer nature an embrace,
while gulls screamed and seals gulped.

"Reverence heals all but that which is
exposed," you said from your heart.
We ignore too much of ourselves —
faults within our quake zones.

I touched a burn on your hand;
salt in my nose puckered my face.
Love dissolves in surf of emotions,
turned into mud by waves and winds

of excess. Understanding was too much
for my skin bag – too much for words.
We drag truth through history to shake
off dust of what isn't true; to understand

what is. I grieve for the rainbow that was
our humanity; for whale, deer, and hawk –
hunted, stripped of skins and plumage
used to symbolize power; their dust, carried

by streams below a sea of stars, watching
as we depart earth, looking for what once
surrounded us – a good life. Each time
a rocket blasts off, more life disappears.

But, as Mark Twain said, "Nothing helps scenery
like ham and eggs," which means, if it enhances
the interests of people, it's OK or as a logging
company Exec summarized, "Try wiping your

ass with an owl." I reflected on Egypt,
now 90% sand; 256 species gone in America.
Am I pissing against the wind of reality?
Being human is a collective deception of life –

what pulls truth together, can also pull it apart.
I worry for the mother raccoon with three babies
who rangers describe as, " . . . very aggressive
and ingenious." Will they be ingenious enough

to survive haranguing by humans; separated
by roads, with scant food, dirty air and water?
No! I confess, I am a bleeding heart liberal –
part of an evolution of something unnatural –

a self-perpetuating insanity called, civilization,
requiring unnecessary necessities. I recall a huge
slab, chain-sawed from a redwood, mounted
like antlers in front of an Esso station, for tourists

to see life comes in second to gas. Recently,
an old Ash was cut to make way for another
Dunkin' Donuts store in Augusta, Maine.
The manager said, "We needed parking;

too many leaves were falling on our cars."
The store closed because one donut shop
was enough for Augusta, and another store
had a drive-thru, closer to city center.

Looking across the expanse of Cape Alava,
seals used the tide to feed, we saw how truth
is tidal; realized how we squander truth
in contrived reality, the imprint of ancestor's

intoxicating delusions infused within us.
A tragic beauty spread before us; sensing
what is sacred, but more so than one God.
My fear is, when I return, there might be

gift shops; plush raccoons with their plush
babies; magnets bearing raccoon images;
T-shirts and bouncy earth balls while, outside,
several telescopes to scan an empty sea.

Did we think prayer or magic could
renew life; locked in cruise; going too fast
to see a collision-course with consequence;
up-ahead, our need for an ambulance

to rush to the scene of our accident;
those of us left alive, stunned, finally
aware of our family, dying before us –
witnesses to the loss of lives we loved.

Where is the Magic?

"The world is its own magic."
-Shunryu Suzuki

I tried keeping an open mind about magic
when I heard the news report three nuns,
clubbed with their statue of the virgin,
by a man who once played trumpet.

Because I lived in a place that went like this:
slaughterhouse alley off Main Street –
dung trails in, blood trails out – Sundays
could not disguise the stink and crying.

Once, when a carnival peep show
came to town, there was a woman
who slapped me because I would not
touch her breasts; then she laid down

with other girls on straw in front of us,
behind a rope, and smoked a Winston
with her pink vagina. Obviously,
she practiced, but there was no magic.

Today, I learned I might have cancer;
I wanted to take off my tired face,
but I kept thinking of those nuns,
and the vagina smoking the Winston.

I have always been keen on magic;
how rose dust belongs to the heart
of the perfume seller; why pheasants shake
ten minutes before an earthquake.

Apartment Dweller

Sitting at this formica table,
like a Saturday matinee,
staring at the bare bulb,

meditating on the pull chain –
dull little brass balls;
mechanically crimped, fluted

thingamabob with dirty string
and a honky-tonk stereo,
"My baby went and left me. . . "

a specific version of hell
in the apartment below.
Outside, a pigeon flaps,

lands on the phone line,
and stares in at me,
iridescent feathers glow

hope. It doesn't wonder
why or write Zen poetry
with institutional overtones.

Bird, music, chain, bulb –
ascending order of what
is all perishable sculpture;

then my eyes fix on it –
such delicate filament,
golden glowing tungsten –

how this hurts; understanding.

Migration

Frost-shriveled vines stripped of leaves,
swallows in clusters fly out from eaves,
like wild dark grapes flung downwind,

harvest departs in seed-packed stomachs.
River water also runs away from winter;
insects escape on leaves of gold, magenta;

twigs and branches spin in frothy eddies.
While song birds' silhouettes climb the sky,
seasoned poets address approaching clouds,

in autumnal robes, refusing winter's shrouds.
Summer's colors bleed out of musty brocades
of milkweed warp, flower woof, frost-edged.

Red stars explode unseen; recessed in the sky,
an orange comet's tail, burns, streams and dies;
birds, musicians to poet's ears, beat south,

tongues chatter of losses, gains, again.

Flesh or Wood

Across fields of fresh snow,
chainsaws buzz and snarl,
ripping up winter silence.

A bitter stink of exhaust
and gas; a saw bites into a tall,
thick oak, beginning to creak,

teeters briefly, crashes onto vines
and ferns. Veins, circles of rings,
laid open to cold air, steam

like intestines on the stump;
the trunk, sympathetic, puzzled
by it's separation, weeps sap;

like any dead body, becomes
cold, rigid. Rings, like braille,
tell of ninety + years of life;

narrow rings, dry years; little
growth – wider rings, wetter
months; more pulp. Eyes closed,

I slide my fingers to the center
of the stump, all rings come
closer to when the tree was

thinner, shorter – new to newer
bark; scars of carved-in lover's
initials, speak of a year of love.

A hole in the sky shows where limbs,
now splayed, broken, once reached
for sun and moon; dropped seed

in a circle below, as wide as her
longest, graceful limbs reached.
Life, so invisible within –

we cannot catch it when it leaves –
wood or flesh, we kill too much.

Medicine Man

Oddly, voice sweating anticipation,
hasty glances watched my reaction.
"We all knew there was a bull in the area,"

he said, saying how a doctor in the hunting party,
a medicine man, swayed side-to-side on brush,
making crunching noise like moose steps, blowing

a plastic cow call. "Charlie shot him; my job
was to winch him on the trailer; I'm not sure
who sawed the antlers off. . . " but there they were,

with part of the skull, on a few bloody newspapers,
on the K-Mart braided rug. "Get it out of the house,"
Greg's wife yelled, but smiling like you might smile

at a boy for bringing a frog into the house. Why he
lugged it in was a mystery – unless to let the head
be present to hear the odd tale of it's death.

Next month, at the fall tribal gathering; trying
to unravel truth from Greg's tale, I found parts
of it for sale in rows of cardboard, vendors' boxes –

real skin faces of fox, coyote, mink, carefully cut off
and sorted by animal – 3-5 bucks each; boxes of bones,
teeth – turtle rattles trimmed with dyed feathers.

The gathering ended when a man, decorated
with feathers, a representative hawk, in a leather
loin cloth, circled the fire; alternately lifting

his feathered leg; admired in heat by four ladies,
in new buckskins, nervously shifting purses,
shoulder-to-shoulder; faces blood-red by firelight.

Something Magnificent

Brittle clumps of broken grass;
bits of stiff brown rope often tied
our captured Indians here;

scattered around the large pine,
small footprints in frozen mud.
A cowboy was shot over there.

My memories begin to unfold;
I discover them like arrowheads,
the bones of undeveloped plots,

days we won and lost the West.

I remember calvary rushing in;
Col. Jack removing his glass eye,
rubbing off ten miles of prairie

dust, while we stared into his empty
socket. Here is where Davey once
played dead, and now really is.

Ears to the ground, we imagined

hearing thunder of horses' hooves,
but only silence hangs in clouds today.
Ghosts of cowboys and Indians

watch me, hunkered down below pines;
rubbing sap on a sore thumb; swearing,
so many memories hanging in cold air,

strung up by that notorious gang, time.
A curious creature, familiar with fields
and stars; scent and taste of cold spring

water; something magnificent; disappearing —
and I think of children in Iraq and Syria —
are they nostalgic for games like ours?

Like us, do they imitate what is on TV –
inoculated from the reality of killing,
by making believe it is make-believe –

and just like we argued, on any given day,
over who would be cowboys or Indians,
do they argue about who will be infidels;

who will play masked freedom fighters;
who will weakly kneel; who will stand;
who will wield the knife to sever whose head?

Do they have favorite places in the sand,
where they put their ears on the ground,
to hear rumble of approaching tanks;

do they have an endless array of ghosts,
from the proxy war that surrounds them –
a gift, paid for by the Russian people,

the USA, and Iran? How can other, better
memories replace scenes of terror that,
for children, must be painful to pretend?

Can sanity be fashioned from this madness;
will children ever have something magnificent
to imitate – so their games can be about

love and peace, of which all religions speak?

First Snow

First snow comes with a rustle
against dry leaves not yet fallen,
etching a definite landscape;
all things appear black and white.

Through a crack in the barn's side,
the pony laid out in dried manure,
brambles in tangled hair of mane
and tail, forms an oriental image.

Through another, wider crack,
white pastures stretch beyond,
to quiet antique hills; gurgling
stream disturbs their silence.

A deer rustles dead, dry leaves;
brittle twigs snap and crack,
following a path it knows,
a gunshot smashes evening.

A delicate, unique snowflake
melts, leaving a soft impression;
it's design floated down to earth,
then disappeared like Christ.

Hearing loud laughter below,
I follow mixed footprints down,
to a brown body sprawled in snow,
rivulets of blood run to the stream;

I walk slowly back to the house.
where mama cat has caught a mouse;
it's squeals of agony finally stop;
the garden murmurs, it's finished.

Standing on my narrow porch,
looking at cords of wood not in,
both hands bitten raw by cold,
a bird circles, twists, and dives.

Inside, a kerosene lamp splutters;
light flirts with flames' shadows;
wind on the wick is a magician,
dousing light with darkness.

Scent of sweet apples, keeping;
fresh sawn pine, curing; woolen
shirt near the stove, drying; a cold
draft slipping between my blankets.

Almost Lost in Time

Helen of Troy, fathered by Zeus, who disguised
himself as a swan, was hatched from an egg;
now the face that launched a thousand ships

is almost lost in time. Her historic beauty,
a famous mix of reality, myth and magic,
along with all arguments regarding what

she did or did not do, and who she did or did
not do it with, dissolving, filtering into smaller
increments of memory, while Marylin Monroe,

whose sultry smile stared down at me from
a calendar rack in the soup aisle, appeared
as if reincarnated. It was a, "Moment,"

with her luxurious face, coveted by many;
long, black, upturned lashes, and familiar
carmine lips, pouting for me, pushing my

basket. I thought of all those Greek gods,
whose counterfeits crumble in temples,
despite conservation efforts, turning into

dust, our shared inheritance. I take nothing
for granted, knowing months are weeks,
weeks are days, and a day, as we all know,

is just twenty-four little hours. I have becom
rusty at things once automatic, like breathing;
a now, unused Black Belt, hangs in my closet.

Watching commodities, like gold and pork
bellies, flux in the marketplace of each day,
it is trite to say time is precious, but if you Google

the most valuable commodity, the winner is time.
We only have a little, and it cannot be saved,
so there's no time like the present to have

the time of our lives, before time is up;
turning us to dust, mixing with the dust
of Helen, Marylin, crumbling Gods,

and dust of their crumbling temples.

Juju

I knew, when you were introduced as Juju,
my luck had changed; if we had been
in a casino, I would have bet the house.

Your green eyes were like magical dice. Then,
after you gave me your hand with the gold
and ruby ring, the rest of that night

was a blur. Driving your black Jaguar,
below the Egyptian stars to Cairo,
while you freshened your fire engine red

lips, slid over beside me, and confirmed my
suspicions. Halfway there we turned around
and drove back to your beach house

in Alexandria. Thinking of that night,
I handed a man on a small traffic island,
two bucks. He held a printed sign, *Need a job –*

will work for food. "I wouldn't be sitting here
if it wasn't for my wife and kids!" I wished
I would have had more to give him,

but I was pushing a blue, folding walker
with wheels, miles from a bank. Anyway, it
wouldn't have mattered at 5:20 pm. It was

hot; his glasses needed cleaning,
but that was the least of his problems.
An open sore on the side of his nose

looked like it was searing into his head.
Two Safeway bags rested on the seat
of my walker. I hadn't tied the string

to keep the bags from falling. I thought
it would be ok, until I hit an uneven
joint in the sidewalk; the bag holding

my Cheerios and bananas, fell off the seat,
ripping open; three compressed vertebrae
screamed, Sit Down! Somewhere! Soon!

20 feet ahead, littered with cups & straws,
a bus stop bench called. I put the bananas
and Cheerios on top of the other bag,

and headed for the bench; my mind flashed
back to Egypt, when I could walk; your green
eyes and perfume; how my luck changed.

Parallel Motion

Leaning into Atlantic, winter sleet,
beating at the rocky, island lane –
shielded by a stone wall, I watch
waves toss froth and seaweed;
listen to boulders grind on
the stone shore, shifted by storm

surge. A green tractor snarls by
in parallel motion; steel and skin
share the narrow lane; pink orchids
watch as wind slaps monoxide,
along with my breath, away.
Kneeling at Saint Enda's well,

where centuries of pilgrims have
worn deep slots into limestone,
my knees rest; I bow my head,
parallel to wherever you are –
walking your dog;
hanging out

your wash; driving down an off-ramp –
walking a steel girder, twenty stories
up; having a beer and barbecue
in your backyard – wondering if
yours are the parallel prayers,
blowing in the wind,

I am hearing?

Part II

"Nothing should ever be treated with contempt.
Whatever it is that lives, a man, a tree, or a bird,
should be touched gently, because the time
is short. Civilization is another word for respect for life."
-Elizabeth Goudge

Understanding, Fifty Miles Northwest of Fairbanks

The large snowy owl in the oak, with golden, piercing eyes –
and six grey wolves, their yellow-green orbs circling firelight,
were not stuffed toys who felt sad for me, hunkered-down by
my fire. They did not come to play – not bored by wilderness
silence – not there to welcome me to Alaska.

Theirs was the same universal hunger shared by a bobcat – ten
years earlier, 3,000 miles south – who stalked me deep into Moss
Hollow, below Rattlesnake Mountain, because the fat squirrel
I shot for supper, was leaking a trail of blood that smelled like
a meal larger than a mouse, or skinny, tick-ridden, rabbit.

I heard Nature tell the bobcat it would be a long winter,
with deep snow; urging her to overcome her hesitation, saying,
"He is only 13." I knew everything when I was 13, so I was certain
Nature was correct when she told me, "Because you only have
a .22, it would be better to leave the squirrel on the next rock,

rather than have you bleed to death, two miles from home." Also,
I knew her weather forecast was true, because the gray squirrel had
built a nest, high in the maple, beside the trail. His high nest meant
deep snow and a desire to survive, which my .22, and the curiosity
of my hunger, had deprived.

Observing behavior in other creatures is essential. Killing
and eating some rabbits, squirrels, a raccoon, one possum
and a few groundhogs, apart from satisfying my curious, young
hunger, helped me see everything struggles to survive –
has to sense when to alter habits –

know where a good chance for food can be found. It's like
a receiver catching a forty-five yard pass – an essential connection
made in a vital moment – a modern display of prowess – fist
pumps signal success. There is a semblance of prowess in sports,
but we no longer speak the original language.

Only shadows of that language survive in people – having lost the
savage dialect long before our mother's mother's mother – around
the time we collectively felt a need to cut our finger and toenails.
Now, when hunger makes us crave satisfaction,
we go to Burgerworld,

where we don't worry about lurching over the edge of a reckless
moment – unless we eat too much grease and salt – which could
hasten our journey to the realm of dust. The pack of circling
wolves, firelight flickering off their yellow-green, averting eyes,
hesitated at the edge of their reckless moment

due to fear of fire, but also fear of light-blindness, and in that
moment of lost vision, to lose their lives, when an easier meal
could be found in daylight; when my movements could be
studied, parlayed by twelve eyes. The snowy owl had a different
story, I was too large to carry off,

and her species doesn't hunt in groups. These are the compatible
and incompatible choices all of us once faced – when humans
knew the need for a honed, second sense; to help us be victorious,
find food – now to attain the corporate advantage. The wolf pack
quickly shared their decision not to attack,

collectively did the math, determined risk, weighed the value
of what might be lost against what could be divided; used their
collective intelligence, and senses, to achieve more than chance,
within a deficiency of natural light; overcome by fire's glare.
The snowy owl could only watch

to see if the wolves failed or succeeded. Everything in nature fights
to survive – staying alert to the possibility for leftovers.
Satisfying hunger requires a flexible palate, but the snowy owl
and wolf pack had to go hungry that night, restless in firelight;
empty stomachs sharpened by hunger through the long night.

I have never felt sorry for any creature who, for whatever
reason, could not manage to devour me. Only after comparing their
hunger to mine, have I felt the sorrow of their empty stomach, but I
was not sorry that night – that night, I watched them watch me.
They might have dozed,

but I did not – not when their impatient teeth or claws, despite
reasoned hesitation, might have risked snagging me for a meal,
in a restaurant where I had no desire to be served as an appetizer,
the main course, or dessert.

When Turtles Called My Name

I remember that day, thick with color of trumpet vine
flowers, blaring their orange invitations of nectar to bees.

Beds of lilies burst with different orange blossoms below,
as though the best of earth was reaching for the best of sky.

I was ten and had wondered down the path from Sam's house,
with the scent of his cracked, corn-cob pipe still in my brain;

Gigi was striking the pan of tomatoes with a spoon, like a dull
dinner gong and, like other afternoons, the turtles waddled out.

Not looking left or right, they converged on her by the chimney
seat where, in a blue print dress – her gray hair a confederacy

of curls – she emptied the pan of tomatoes onto a china plate.
Turtles craned their necks in, grabbing at chunks of red pulp;

one, orange and black box turtle, looked up at her, his leathery
neck, arched, swaying, and I understood what he was saying.

This was the first time I heard the language of animals,
and I knew I could never consider people unique again.

Later, fat raindrops fell wide apart, like splats of butter;
I greased my skin briskly with brown soap, and frothed

as rain thickened; swollen, cold drops fell through hot air,
making small streams of soap slide down my dark skin,

off my feet, leaving me like a flower growing from
a puddle, rising out of many, small iridescent bubbles;

then I ran under the rain spout to rinse, and listen to turtles
call my name from their homes under wet, green, lily leaves.

I remember the clean scent of trumpet flowers after rain,
beaded with silver drops, their veined, orange beauty magnified.

From shedding Sycamore bark, dotted with dry husks of locusts;
from a harmony of insects, swarming after the storm;

from a mosquito drawing blood from my thin arm, bloated,
I learned to be small, in that moment when I had felt so big.

Last Night's Dream

Last night I dreamed I was in high school again
and whoever Ron Lawn is, called me a *Door
Master,* meaning I can fill a concert venue
to perform my songs; he also said
he admired my work.

I had never heard of the term *Door Master,*
but teenagers there were in wonder
and awe which must mean they knew
who Ron Lawn was.

I know they were in wonder and awe
by the way they suddenly began using crayons
with panache and brio so I reasoned it was
okay to be a *Door Master* if they were
drawing great pictures.

I was surprised they were using crayons
in High School, but then I thought,
maybe this was part of the dumbing-down
of America. Besides, I was on my way

to the office to get a copy of my schedule
because I couldn't remember which room
I was supposed to be in for which class,
and because I was 72, I wanted to know
why I was still in High School.

But I was happy, and none of the other students
seemed to be concerned I was there, which made
me wonder if I was part of the dumbing-down
and just didn't know it?

However, since I had a high credit score
and knew where the cafeteria was
it was ok for me to be happy, especially since
other students were cool with everything,
but I was concerned

because I couldn't find something in the pouch
on my rolling walker, but teachers were amazed
at how much stuff I could stash there,
so it all seemed good.

Activity suddenly switched to the gym which,
next to the cafeteria, was my favorite place
in High School. I was hopping around
like I was 16 again which did make me
wonder how, at 72, I could be like

16, but I'm not good at math, so I stopped
thinking about it. My life, then, had a Zen-
like aspect which reassured me everything
was as it should be.

Gym teachers were delighted I could
leap over rows of folding chairs and,
like the kids finding out I was a *Door Master,*
admiration showed in the teachers' eyes.
I can't go far without my walker

so suddenly jumping over chairs made life
cool, but then I woke up, which was a shock –
not to be in the gym. I tried going back
to sleep, to find out what was next, but by then

it was morning, so I switched on the weather,
adjusted my recliner, and settled back into being 72.

Monday Night Barking

Although I no longer have a sore throat,
I open a crinkly-wrapped drop, tossing
it at my tonsils; a few minutes later,
I am thinking about winter.

Menthol reminds me, ice relieves pain,
so I get a cube and slide it over my eyelids,
dreaming of falling snow; without knowing
why, I begin craving a wet summer.

The mind is a fickle thing that makes sense
only when you climb inside and see
it doesn't know where it is going –
like riding in a car with no driver.

It must be like this to be terminally ill –
to imagine going somewhere, foot hard
on the accelerator, but the speedometer
hanging on zero. Autumn officially begins

on Saturday. The ex-marine across
the street, keeps yelling at his ex-wife,
which starts their Alsatian barking,
but I still leave the window open.

Nothing seems to matter more than usual;
my breathing revs like a racing engine.
Now I know how pigs can become alcoholics;
why dogs in medieval days wore suits of armor.

March Blizzard, Maine

Gas lamps softly glow; the transistor
warns of white-outs; gives locations
of warming shelters. Is the skunk under
the porch in a dry corner; are the wild

cats in the barn; the great owl, huddled?
My windows are drummed by snow
and sleet. The only scent is old, burned
toast; wind has shifted to the northeast.

The only way out is with a shovel,
but there will be no mail, so I open a can
of beans and sit in my rocker, wrapped
in a cocoon of wool and cotton.

Low on stove wood, water to prime
the pump will come from snow, melted
on the gas range. Built in 1847, from local
trees, the house creaks; leaking wind flutters

shades; rattles old windows. A seven foot
drift by the porch will require a loader.
I light a lantern to check the chickens,
gather a few eggs, then go to bed early,

in darkness, listening to wind. Dropping
snow plow clunk; jangling chains at 3 am,
like Marley, wakes me; gusts slam the house;
waiting in my linen cave until dawn.

The Deer

The second day of November,
I saw a deer head on a smoking
dump; a burned tin can lay

near the deer's singed eye.
Fall rain fell heavy, pelting
the down white hide

that once leaped wild over
red summer sun rays. An ear
stood straight up, listening

to my shout; an eye, aimed
in my direction, looked
to see if the same would

happen to me. I looked
at a quiet heart lying near
a Hawaiian punch can,

and slashed lungs on top
a pickle jar; I looked at two
knobs where antlers had been

sawed off – then I left
that brown head, among
the burned and burning

town trash, slowly turning
to ashes, and washing away
in rain. Halloween crepe

caught my eye, and a crack,
my ear, splintering silence.

Mice in My Mind

In our cabin that spring,
when I was sixteen, mice had
survived by gnawing a bar

of dry, white soap; sleeping
in a bureau drawer, nested
in bunches of red and green

fuzz, chewed off the rug;
newspaper shreds, and woven
strands of Jill's auburn hair.

I thought my life was not
so different from the mice –
just different things to chew

on; human, thanks to luck.
Looking back, I see I moved
through everything too fast,

brushing too much aside
as unacceptable; not having
learned much from the mice,

now ghosts, happy to gnaw
at my memories, like they are
a bar of dry soap; using fuzzy

stuff in my brain as a nest.

Columbus Day

Afternoon sun sifts through mottled leaves
of a large oak; three yellow leaves just let
go, twisting to the ground; a Bluejay bitches
in the upper branches, while another Jay,

it's mate, screams back from a nearby
spruce; it's a great day! Some of the cattails,
on the edge of the duck pond are split open,
what looks like beige fudge, oozes out.

Voices from a boy and girl, trying to fly kites,
drift over the large, grassy field. A sign reads,
private property, but red leaves from shrubs
fall anyway. I've circled the pond three times,

it's too nice to go inside. Sunlight, spread
across water, reflects on overhanging limbs
and leaves, so it looks like they are the source
of shimmering light, but then two red leaves

let go, land on water, sending out little ripples,
scrambling light into a sort of yellow melange.
Today reminds me of a day in Maine and,
Eileen, who fashioned steps up to her porch,

by using three red bricks, pushed together; a large
wooden box, then a tall chair. The day after I saw
her, while carrying groceries up to her porch, she
had slipped off the chair. A dog in her yard

kept barking. She hit her head on the bricks.
Her son lived about a half-mile away. She
had told me he was manager of a paper mill
and had a family; she didn't want to bother him.

That was Columbus Day; after seeing her make-
shift steps, I asked her to use the back door until
I could find a volunteer to make new steps. She said
ticks in the high grass, by the back door, scared her.

The card I gave her, with my name and number,
was still in her jacket pocket. I told the EMT
her son lives a half-mile away. I heard him pass
the message to police, standing nearby,

their emergency radios crackling, cutting
in and out, while in the background, the dog
kept barking as if it was yelling, let me in;
sounds of everyone trying to find a way.

Alaska Wilderness

In Northern Quebec, René Richard drew art from life
using crayon, pencil and chalk, on wrinkled
sheets of meat paper,

of firelight reflecting on men, tents, and sled dogs.
Chalk was snow and birch trees – flames were yellowish
paper with dashes of red crayon – chalk,

ashes; all else was penciled-in. My tent is a canvas tonight,
painted by shadows and flickering flames. Beyond
the perimeter of light, snow crunches –

crunches some more – then stops. I cannot draw
a picture of how this make me feel, wishing
the fire would stop spitting

sap and sparks; my ears stop pushing their limits – straining
to separate, understand sounds. Have you ever
been to a distant place,

where the end of your world feels like the moment you are in;
where you drink ice, chopped from a river
with an ax, then melted

in a pan over flames, cooled into sweet, thin sap;
surrounded by earth, frozen into hummocks,
resembling ant hills, and you are alone

on tundra, a small creature, weaving a way through?

Steave and the Rambler

My brother Steave coveted the '57 Rambler coupe on Rt. 27,
with it's rust-colored body and remaining hints of original green –
a cream top that, in his opinion, was reasonably clean – with
a dent over the driver's side, easily popped out.

It had been four years since he first saw it, near the edge
of the road, emerging with a new crop of dandelions
from ice and snow. It didn't matter if it had to be pulled out
of six + years of orchard grass, and tangled weeds –

a minor problem or that the body required about five tubs
of Bondo; a rear panel; one taillight and back bumper, gone.
His buddy Mike, or Billy, sympathetic, understanding souls,
both with trucks, trailers, and strong backs,

would help him get the pieces home. It would be worth it!
The fact that a Willy's convertible, with it's big-block, Buick V-8,
occupied the only bay in Steave's barn, was not an obstacle; even
if his yard, full of vehicles, and stuff that might be useful

down the road, was way past overflowing. A Town Selectman,
who had to first get past Sophie, Steave's Dingo dog, suggested
he might have to apply for a junkyard license. The official
would be stalled, or Steave might, strategically,

not be home. If worse came to worse, it would mean he had to sell
something, which would have been like pulling his own molar,
using vise grips; with no anesthetic. The Rambler might have
to wait in the field another year, where he would watch it,

making sure it was safe until spring – a price already dickered
with the owner, who almost let him cover it with a tarp.
The Rambler stayed there for two more years; Steave stalled
the owner, telling him he was close to having space in his yard,

and a truck strong enough to pull the Rambler out. That car
was like one of his kids, waiting for an empty room, so she
could come home. The owner, after three town warnings,
and trying to reach Steave by phone, had it hauled off.

His dream of restoring it, after winning Megabucks, didn't
pan out, so when Steave came along, he decided it was
time to let her go. What the owner didn't know,
was Steave had banked on winning Megabucks;

the Rambler was part of his dream, of it all coming true.

Part III

"I helped in the raping of half a dozen Central American republics for the benefit of Wall Street. I helped purify Nicaragua for the International Banking House of Brown Brothers in 1902-1912. I brought light to the Dominican Republic for the American sugar interests in 1916. I helped make Honduras right for the American fruit companies in 1903. In China in 1927 I helped see to it that Standard Oil went on its way unmolested. Looking back on it, I might have given Al Capone a few hints. The best he could do was to operate his racket in three districts. I operated on three continents."— *Gen. Smedley D. Butler,* a Marine, and Medal of Honor recipient, from his book, "War is a Racket."

"The political and commercial morals of the United States are not merely food for laughter, they are an entire banquet." -*Mark Twain*

Civilization

For Anny Fenton

Last night, a nine year old Belfast girl was shot
in her home. The paper said it was a mistaken
killing; she bled to death on her jigsaw puzzle.

Her father gone, her mother deaf and dumb,
Barbara McAlorum had learned sign language.
The INLA expressed regret saying, " . . . she was

the wrong target," which didn't surprise me,
coming from a fully developed victim culture,
where any criminal with a lawyer can be a victim.

A ten year old once explained, matter of factly,
". . . civilization is where stuff happens."
When she told me this, in a wilderness,

propped stiffly against a white birch, it was raining;
she wanted to go shopping, because the earth
was turning muddy around her small boots.

I couldn't help thinking of what she said when
my TV blinked, flashing Barbara's former face –
how life resembles a collage of contrasts – stuff

pasted-in childishly, one tiny image with another,
making a big picture filling a humungous page
with the strong scent of a suspicious glue.

If I were Japanese, I could take this pungent collage,
divide, cut, and fold it into a thousand cranes,
and call the space of time it took to fold them,

peace. Together, we could build a shelter
in which to keep the thousand birds;
a candle could be kept lit in perpetuity

for Barbara, civilization, and the INLA.
After a millennium or two of burning wax,
the odor of glue could mellow into a perfume –

similar to the way the waxy scent
in early cathedrals can be mistaken
for a civilized odor.

Guatemala City – Belfast, N.I.

Well past curfew we left the bar,
after looking there for Randy,
when a death squad in a black

Lincoln Town Car, rolled up beside us,
windows tinted dark; nothing visible
inside. The street was empty;

one a.m. air, hot and sticky – thick
with stink of lingering fear; too much
new death hanging in stale air.

Did the CIA pay extra for tinted glass
on the Lincoln; were we
about to be grabbed,

like Guatemalans – beaten, and shot;
disfigured bodies dumped in a ravine –
disappeared; leaving wives, mothers,

searching? In my left eye, I saw our hotel;
in the right one, the driver's window
beside me, matched

our speed. "Don't stop; keep walking
slowly and look straight ahead,"
I said quietly.

They stayed beside us, windows rolled up,
almost to the corner where, without
stopping, they slowly

rolled off into darkness. We turned left,
walking a little quicker toward our hotel
lights, not looking back.

The central police station, a bad local joke,
was on a hill above us; inside our hotel,
a journalist from El Salvador hid.

Ten years earlier, behind Richard's home
in Belfast, well past curfew, I had
watched a black sedan stop

under a street lamp; two men pulled a third
man out of the car, and began
hitting him with their rifle

butts, until he lay quiet by the bumper.
I went to jump across the ditch
to stop them, but Richard

grabbed my arm, and said, "That is what
they want you to do. If you go, you
won't come back." In long seconds

that followed, I felt the depth of darkness
and hate; thick air carried the stink of fear,
new death – like the night,

beside the black Lincoln. How similar
both nights were, with death choking oxygen
out of the air; giving me an idea,

how it would feel to not come back.

After Nicaragua

"Fear paralyzes all efforts to succeed."
-Yogananda

For several months, after returning from Nicaragua,
a dark voice on the other end of my phone,
pronounced, we're coming for you at midnight!
Why midnight, I asked, I might miss you
in my sleep –

a long silence would follow, then the phone went dead.
It was funny when my trash bags were taken a few times,
and not returned. When they called, I asked if they found
anything interesting, but heavy silence
was always their reply.

One night, when they called, a chopper was landing.
I remember thinking, this is America, I shouldn't fear
my government, but it was 1987, and I did –
what protects freedom, protects covert plans
and their operatives.

The putrid smell of a hospital for amputees, near Matagalpa,
still haunted my mind; the fifteen year old child soldier
who handed me the landmine shard that took his leg;
printed on the jagged, olive-green fragment, were letters
of words, . . de in the USA.

The boy, a victim of America's proxy war with the USSR,
had become part of their propaganda, with no royalties
except the shard and stump of his leg. Meanwhile, back
in the USA, war mongers prepared to invade Nicaragua;
Smedley Butler rolled in his grave;

the CIA, not content to just watch Nicaragua be bled,
joined in. At a peace rally on the Boston Common, I found
myself nose-to-nose with a young, American Marine,
who barked at me that he was going to Nicaragua,
to cut off someone's ears,

and mail them to me. I told him to go home, cut off
his mother's and father's ears, and mail those. He got this
crazy look in his eyes, like he was trying not to believe me –
clenching and unclenching his fists – trying to
decide which to use first,

but then he turned and stalked away. When the voice
called, the night after the rally, I said, Come and kill me,
if you think you can; cut out my tongue, burn or bury it,
someday there will be peace, if only
in our silence.

Red

Many Saturday nights, armed with overnight passes,
we caught a bus for the bright lights of Seattle,
where we began drinking

at the upper end of Pike, working our way
through bars along the street. Three-quarter's
way down, three-quarter's way drunk,

Red would sometimes take out his top plate,
toss it up, then run around, trying
to catch it in his mouth.

He always missed, but despite being wasted,
and laughing like a fool, he would somehow
snag it, one-handed.

After it hit the sidewalk, twice, and shattered,
the CO told Red if he broke them again,
he would give him an Article 14,

but it didn't stop him from trying once more.
Red died in Vietnam, but I still see
his red hair; his face

looking up at his pink plate, turning slowly
in the night air; our laughter
rolling down Pike.

Cherry Blossoms

pink

dangling

upside down

umbrella petals

shed cold scented

tears of spring rain

drops on me

The Mailboat

Flung from the cargo deck, hawsers were made fast
fore and aft; boatmen corralled the bullish, rust-blue
ship, trying to mount the quay.

Bags of Polish coal, I misread as, polished; stacked
alternately on groaning, splintering pallets; off-
loaded in rope cradles, creaked with complaints.

The raucous bitching of wet rope, pinched by a winch,
protested, while hawsers thumped the starboard
side, upbraiding the rising and falling sea.

Two dogs, not sure what they were seeing,
looked up repeatedly for their master's approval,
until shooed off from sniffing three, debarking

passengers. Then, like an invasion of Norsemen,
cold sleet attacked until we had to turn away;
all but the boatmen fled for home, or the pub.

Angry March weather, with almost biblical ferocity,
did not relent for two days, with sleet, afterward,
in stone crevices.

Early morning of the third day, storm spent,
the big ship set sail, leaving only heavy breath
from the sea; boulders shifted on the western side,

some weighing one-hundred tons; torn golden locks
of seaweed; shafts of sea rod and other wrack,
to be gathered, sorted, stacked and dried.

Finally blown out, that storm is remembered
by two births, one boy and one girl;
a death, and this poem.

House on Inis Oírr

Like a rite, the black bull near O'Brien's Castle
bellowed from his hillock again this morning
at the two brown cows in their small field below.

Several roosters were doing their best to call
all hens to attention as a dark cloud marched by;
drumming sleet turned a window into a snare.

I searched for red coals; though the fire was cold,
raked clinkers yielded two; small, singing birds,
flew toward an aqua sea; three beached Curraghs.

Perished by the cold, I put on the kettle for tea,
and rubbed my hands together, which proved useless,
so like the world and his wife, I buttered

the bread. After my tea, I scraped at the back
boiler where clumps of thick soot, blacker than
bats, dropped off in sticky clusters.

A fire soon had radiators chattering.
Cottage walls, three feet thick, harbored
more stories than a dozen sailors could tell.

For well over a hundred and fifty years
those walls witnessed birth and death;
creatures, inside for winter, complaining.

Bull and roosters finally gone quiet,
sun was trying it's hand at a window;
turned a white donkey, outside, golden.

Over grey limestone cracks and crevices,
frog, bee orchids, and heathers; white moths
in the sun, fluttered toward a quiet, green sea.

Eve of the Feast of St. Brigid

from, Carmina Gadelica

Inside, a turf fire will glow, mounded in a grate;
a bed of rushes or straw will be made for the Brideóg.

The Brideóg doll will be decorated with ribbons and shells;
she will be attended through the night by young women.

On the day of the feast, the Brideóg will be carried house-
to-house; crosses for Brigid will be woven from rushes;

they shall not be cut by iron, but pulled by hand; gathered
in silence; brought out in preparation, on the eve of the feast.

A cross placed in the rafters will keep the roof from flying
off a house in a storm, and keep away mischievous

fairies. Butter and milk, however scarce, will be prepared;
the feast will be of tea, milk, boxty or oatcakes. For luck,

last year's, now dried, brown cross can be fed to livestock;
planted with the first potato or scattered over the land for a good

crop. A strip of ribbon or cloth, blue is best, pinned outside
by the door, will be blessed by the Saint on the eve of the feast

as she travels over the Isle; a piece cut from the ribbon
or cloth and placed on an injury or illness, will bring a cure.

"On the day of Bríde of the white hills

The noble queen will come from the knoll

I will not molest the noble queen,

Nor will the noble queen molest me."

Glencree Night

Striking a wooden match, sulfur
scented the cottage air; three candles
spluttered, settled into a soft glow.

Turf from the bog burned orange
in your grate; you offered a place
on your hearth, near fire's warmth,
flames flickered shadows on walls;

then the baby, murmuring, woke us.
Slipping quietly from your bed,
whispering, placing your hand in his

crib, you quieted him; fire's weakened glow
still lit the room. Then, early morning sound
of hooves made me rise; out the window,
seven wild goats, stamping, by the holly;

led by a horned, white-bearded billy.
Rain and sleet beat at the thatch roof;
old window frames rattled with wind.

Goats, like they were hypnotized, stared
in at me, until turning, all together, they
bolted through the gate, into the gully.
In morning light you nursed the baby.

A hundred years of memories lodged in
walls around us, called out – wakes, parties,
matchmaking and dancing, ". . . 'round the

house and mind the dresser;" laughter,
sweet pipe smoke; boiling splutter of pots
of spuds; cries of newborns; cows, long ago,
inside for winter, complaining; fiddles' strings,

lingering on notes of slow airs; farewells
to immigrant kin, while below the hearth,
hollow cow skulls, buried under large flag

stones, echoed rhythmic sounds of past
dancers; repeated jig and hornpipe steps.
Later, saying our goodbyes, we held each
other close, knowing we would hold dear,

memories of that time, lit by candles' glow;
the baby, now thirty years old, at your breast.

Dear Ants

I am amazed by such a long ticket line,
wending its way through my living room;
so many of your friends and family, headed
for my kitchen counter where, with your

sense of smell or by reading my mind,
you found my new jar of honey, now
using it as a food concession for your
spontaneous festival. You must have

sent out many texts and tweets. A band
is setting up, using my box of tea bags
as a riser, and place from which to sell
tees, CD's, and other band merch;

a head-shop with miniature glass, made
locally, is near the band and, in strobes,
I see many couples copulating. I'm sure
that's marijuana in the air! Unfortunately,

I had to call the police, otherwise the world,
his wife, and their cousins, would quickly
be arriving, so I apologize for having to break-
up the festival, but you must surrender my jar

of honey, send the musicians home, and shut
down the vendors. I will be quick! Of course,
smoke the rest of your joints, and finish making
love – far be it from me to stop free love –

but next time, please mind the no trespassing sign!

Part IV

"There are only two ways to live your life: one is as though nothing is a miracle; the other is as though everything is a miracle."
-Albert Einstein

Porn Poem for Emily

*"It's not the load that breaks you
down — it's the way you carry It."*
-Lena Horne

A young New York poet recently
proclaimed in a poem, "Porn
is Free!" But what would you do,
Emily, if the fairy tale wolf came
to life, and snatched the Little Red
Riding Hood of your dreams?

Porn is the casual observation
of younger and younger women,
tied up, tied down, blind folded –
upside down, sideways, backwards
for cameras, and for you, watching
while they get stuff stuffed in them –

like gagging for your pleasure.
At what point do we have mercy
and stop watching those gross
performances? One million pages
of porn on the web, twenty years
ago – am I nostalgic for less reality?

Video 357864 seemed to define
how a young woman could become
ultimate raw hamburger in a Cadillac,
wearing a glittering pendant for the initial
of her first name – unless "G" was her
stage name, so to speak. Oh how it

banged like a shutter in a storm on her
little breasts. In a Netflix documentary,
little gets paid extra, but look who's
tossing rocks at the glass house –
the same guy who, without the web,
used to sneak in Playboy. Footsteps

in the long hallways of night could
be angels, ashamed and humiliated,
uncertain if the problem is them,
us, or both – everything devolving
into a smaller vision of the universe;
our sisters and brothers, lured into

unrelenting darkness. Regurgitating on
YouTube, a guy set a record eating bacon
wrapped in bacon; as of yesterday, 100,000
views of a woman, on surveillance, pissing
on a door mat. What a strange trip,
from depicting a hunt on cave walls,

into porn; from driving 75 miles to sell
a pint of blood, only to get there and learn
they just stopped buying? That was Maine,
1967; I had 38 cents for gas to get home
before darkness; an approaching blizzard.
Why does porn make life feel like Pompeii,

Emily, just dying to be buried again?

Refugees on TV

Hungarian police on TV are pushing back
hundreds of refugees who are pushing police,
back, trying to get people they love to safety.

Refugees have shock on their faces, that batons
and angry police are their greeting, after fleeing
in overloaded boats; walking hundreds of miles

into the unknown; paying, "guides," to get through
dangerous places, as if they were on safari in Africa,
but without amenities and creature comforts –

aware there are lions, tigers, and dangerous men
waiting in the bush to rob and charge them, just
to get to a place with a wall of angry faces. A boy

about ten, shouts, " They don't care we are hungry?"

It reminded me of a refugee camp in Guatemala,
where hundreds of children were forced into
a fenced-in area, with slab wood outhouses;

one cold-water faucet. Huts had dirt floors; kids
tossed a makeshift ball of knotted, dirty rags,
their dry hair an odd shade of orange; their eyes,

like these refugees' eyes, now staring from the TV;
aware they exist through the kindness of others
which, at the worst time, like milk, can sour.

Trump, a statue of hopelessness, accuses all refugees
of being members of ISIS trying to invade America,
while many thousands – most, helpless children,

wait, homeless and hungry in his privileged shadow;
not in need of a translator to understand Trump's jowls
sucking the wind from their hope. A barbed wire divide

is like a badminton net; on one side, a few police toss little
bags of food from a grassy knoll, over the fence, at thousands
of reaching hands. A few bags fall into mud, where refugees

scramble to grab them. This is the scene used for a fade-
away shot, making everything a contiguous blur of people,
fence and mud, with Trump's obnoxious voice, overriding

everything, snarling, "We gotta suspect these people!"

Desert Museum Docent

The blond docent with peckish eyes
stared into mine, then at her flower;
Smell it honey, she said, holding it

up to my nose. It's like watermelon
I replied. I think so too, she drawled, her blue
western eyes shooting at my eastern chest.

On the way to the museum this morning,
approaching Miracle Mile Road, a boy
in a red T-shirt lay dead on the Tucson road;

several cars had pulled over; a guy with a big,
overhanging gut, wearing dirty cowboy boots,
waved us on. A straw hat lay near the boy's head.

Looking down, there were beads of sweat
on the docent's breasts; I kept thinking
of the boy, face-down on asphalt, 103 degrees.

When the docent saw my eyes fixed
on her breasts, her tan legs flexed; I could
see her toes wiggle in her white canvas

shoes. Standing in her shadow, my son
escaped the heat of her voice; her Siren
eyes, almost lured me behind a Saguaro.

Later, headed home on Oracle Drive,
I saw her in a red Chevy, wearing shades,
top down, gunning it when the light

turned green; her Aqua Net hair glistened
in the evening sun, strands shining like
steel; stiff enough to take on a twister.

Hey, my son said, Isn't that the lady?
Yep! That's her, I answered, feeling
holes in my eastern chest, leaking.

The Prize

The final prize documents proclaimed,
LOUIS will win One Million Dollars;
my name in bold caps – winning
numbers issued *exclusively* to me,
contained in a convincing manila

envelope. I signed the, *On-Location
Approval Form for TV,* permitting
the prize patrol to appear at my door,
and Dave to shout, "Congratulations,
Louis!" over barking neighbors' dogs.

There were the usual gazillion coupons,
printed in stinky inks, for cooking oil, cat
food and gadgets; there was an open
window on the envelope, showing my
order stamps; a glossy, simulated photo

of my back read, "I can't believe it!
I guess I'm rich now!" That did not sound
like me, so I began to worry. All I could see
was the back of a head that looked like
it had a beard and pony tail, but the clothes

concerned me, I do not own an Elizabethan
waistcoat. A special coupon offered a car –
a Range Rover or Jag – I chose the Rover
in British Green, and considered buying
the double, Patsy Cline CD's, for luck,

but didn't. I did sign the *Release Authorization,*
allowing Tom Brokaw, of NBC News, to show
me winning on national TV. I pasted all
stickers in their places, considered a magazine
about the Civil War, but went for one I could

cancel and still keep the Chinese radio.
It has been two months now, but no sign
of Dave or the Prize Patrol; my cat watches
a bird on the railing; a python can go
for as long as six months without eating.

Translating a Dream of Death

Last night, I was the Poet, Apollonius, dreaming in Greek;
reincarnated in Hillsboro, Oregon. I had the entire Library
of Alexandria, the Internet, at my fingertips. Hippocrates
was sitting beside me in a Ramada Inn, on cushy pillows,
administering a warm glass of Jack Daniel's Black Label,
with a teaspoon of honey from the Isle of Ikaria.

Within this dream, I saw a shoal of iridescent, flying fish,
take flight through incandescent moon glow; stars, jeweled,
inset eyes of Uranus, radiant cut, shimmered; effervesced
in a cobalt sky, watching me as I departed the Ramada
to board the Argo, where my voice became infused
with timbers, hewn from the sacred forest of Dodona.

Just before dawn, assisted by Nyx, goddess of night, my journey
to Hades began. The Argo, with me shivering in her timbers,
laden with exotic spices, sank, flavoring the water on our way
down. I implored the help of Hades while, to fish swimming by,
I explained the essence of spice, using the dialect of cardamon,
which I learned in Miss Phipps' third grade class.

Within my dream, myriad fish dreamed in anise, cinnamon
and cloves; through the moonlit water, like blue gauze above,
in water stained by saffron, vanilla and lavender scented,
scary Octopi scooted by, with black peppercorn glares
in their eyes, exhaling cinnamon breath; their eight arms
mixing, and remixing, a hip-hop sort of mash-up of spices.

The next morning, I realized nothing is as difficult
to translate as a dream, where there is usually more
than one language, with several meanings. However,
most dreams, if given enough time, translate themselves,
so I went to a candy shop for breakfast. I thought a tooth
was saying, feed me, but it was saying, fill me! Using

the language of pain, the tooth explained my mistake.

Red, Spiral-Bound Notebook

At five am, within a dew-soaked dawn, a spiral-
bound notebook, it's red cover and pages oddly
dry, lay on a diesel-soaked path in the train yard,
the word, "Alien," on page one. Was it a warning?

Below the word, Alien, a stick-figure with a big head;
a stick dog beside him – why are aliens men, I wondered?
Hollywood, like an Instagram, appeared in my mind.
A pen lay by the notebook so, like a scribe, I described

a red-leafed tree; Celtic, intertwined images of sparrows,
in yellow, frost-burned shrubs; a distant hammer beat
the dawn air; the horizon like a long, pink tongue, licked
at the sun, like half a lollipop, pulling the other half up.

Down Pleasant Street, beside the health food store, a thorny
shrub with red berries shouted, pay attention, to a maple tree,
mottled by orange remains of summer; acrid skunk scent
burned the air; bachelor buttons, dizzy neon-blue. I listened

to a train horn, or was it the trumpet voice of a swan?
Betty's yard burst with silken milkweed pods; a few
maple seeds helicoptered down, invading early light;
shadows of trees loomed; a warp and weft of fall colors.

A short steel bolt, shined by tires, was geologically pressed
into asphalt at the corner of Pleasant and North. I wondered
if my double, in a double of this town, saw the same things
within his doubled dimension; gazing down a similar,

Sunday street; grasped a duplicate red notebook, below bread
factory vents, absent the scent of bread; past the lumber yard,
not far from Tony's old apartment, the vacant, bakery thrift
shop; one fluorescent strip lighting empty shelves; fat

scent of doughnut grease, once filling crisp air, missing
from the air. The distant hammer pounded my head
into a brutal ache. Walking back toward Center Street,
I wondered aloud, if Lady Luck had deserted town?

The sound of my voice startled three sparrows out
of their shrub. At six am, the last words I wrote were:
"Is my double writing the same things, in a red, spiral-
bound notebook, within his duplicate morning; a green

Vette winding up in first gear, down his Pleasant Street;
Lady Luck fled town; his coffee shop closed for Sunday?"

Paradise

"The only paradise is paradise lost."
-Proust

Spring

Cherry buds

Fresh bark

Lime ferns

Last snow lick

Summer

White petal circles

Bruised grass scent

Baby apples

Baby animals

Fall

Torn green apples

Fragrant wounds

Colder nights

Then listen

Winter

Touches part

Of us that

Hates being touched

By this much loss.

To Lee, Ki Bok

We gazed through pink cherry blossoms
at the mountain where your ancestors
are buried, standing, looking east;
then we went to your parent's home,

in the neon city of Seoul, where
like Romans, we sat and slept on charcoal
heated floors. The next day, my teacher,
I yanked you, a 6th Dan Black Belt,

from the path of a taxi. Back from the dead,
you laughed and said, "A fly swatter can also
be the fly." Taxi drivers could kill four people
before losing their license; you would have

made number two. His taxi, a homemade
jeep with a wooden floor, had a body beat
out of steel oil drums, brush-painted carmine
red; a windscreen cut from green, window glass.

Tonight, fifty years later, peepers in the pond
below, I wonder if they brought you home,
from that bleeding jungle in Vietnam; are you
in that mountain, standing by your ancestors,

looking east; cherry blossom petals drifting
into dusk crevices, where sky meets earth?

My Last Walk

Large grey clouds bleed softly into elegant white
cumulous; pink spring flowers above scurrilous
mosses, radioactive green, underscore a row

of trimmed-back, stubby brown shrubs, prickled
through by slender lemongrass shoots; rows of small
trees above, covered with deliciously pink

flower clusters. A fresh scarlet hue enrobes pruned
rose stems where, during the night, freshly delivered
baby leaves appeared; mosses on stones resemble

miniature bonsais'. Nearby, pale green leaves
also appeared on shrubs last night, like tiny
boutonnieres, ready for the prom – spring's

special night. Walking through an avenue of gray
birch, bark crusty with warts where limbs once
grew, rings of varied, spongy mosses, vibrate

cyan-green, shimmering so neon, surrounding
the base of each birch. Brown brittle twigs, blown
off, along with thousands of last years's dry leaves,

litter new grass like dull confetti, leftover from
a wedding, scattered around; picked through
for this year's nests. New shoots of things,

nameless, but despite my ignorance, here
to dance. It's a great day for everything to be
so alive. It isn't difficult saying goodbye

to winter, seeing new white buds decorate shrubs;
hiding leaves with edges frost-burned brown, that will
shrivel, fall off and drop to the ground. I will miss

the scent of everything newly arrived, pushing musty
odors of winter aside; overcome with awe, standing
near the entrance to the womb of spring, open 24/7,

delivering a steady stream of new shapes, colors, scents
and sounds, faster than I can write them down, trying
to describe what I have so happily found, but feeling

helplessly in awe, like spring, when I merge with love.

Together

*" . . . so intimate that when
I fall asleep your eyes close."*
-Pablo Neruda

Imagining
holding you
works best if
at the same time
you imagine
holding me –

the only thing
better would be
to open our eyes
at the same time
and wake up
together

Part V

"Good to eat, and wholesome to digest, as a worm to a toad, a toad to a snake, a snake to a pig, a pig to a man, and a man to a worm"
- *Ambrose Bierce*

The Worms of Walden

Everything I am going to tell you began with ordering worms for my compost heap. When they arrived, stamped on the two white containers, in bold, black letters, were the words, Concord, Massachusetts. The night they arrived was moonlit, damp and warm, so I left the containers near the compost pile which the worms would call home in the morning.

Around eleven that night, I heard something inside me go off like an alarm clock, telling me to go outside, which I immediately did, and there they were, the Concord worms, escaping through the breathing holes of their plastic containers. When I heard them singing a jovial song of civil disobedience, I realized I might have to deal with a difficult compost pile.

I had images of the compost being drilled by the worms to recall nutrients from the aid of the plants, commanding a general revolution in the garden. As I began picking the worms up and putting them back into their containers, I could hear them talking about their past home beside Walden Pond. It was then the penny dropped, and I realized these were not ordinary worms – these were Walden worms.

I had read a story once, written by a woman descended from Thoreau, who lied near Walden, telling how Thoreau spent much of his two years, two months, and two days at the pond, talking with birds and other creatures. Today, this would be taken as a sure sign a person had lost it, but back then it was considered reasonably normal behavior, unless you only talked with animals or spoke to them while in the company of people.

For those who have no concept of talking with animals, nature communicates everything as a sort of humming vibration – similar to the sound of a refrigerator, but lower. Most Tibetans grow up understanding this vibration, calling it, Om; chanting Om as part of their meditation.

Others have called it, quantum communication – a sort of mental, "Blue Tooth," through which we can communicate with everything in the universe and, conversely, everything can communicate with us. Anyone interested can read about, *Findhorn*.

When I realized the worms were from Walden, I became more interested in their conversation so, after putting them back in their containers, and placing them in a larger, deeper pan, I sat down to listen to them squabble..

After they had complained about their failed escape and argued over who had talked loudly enough to be overheard, I asked the worms about their lives at Walden, and if their ancestors had any connection with Thoreau. They became very excited and said they would tell me an interesting story, if I would grant four requests, which were:

– to use a garden fork to turn the compost pile, but only after 24 hours advance notice;
– to be fed a mixture of table scraps, preferably with no oil or fat, at least once a week;
– to be given a gallon of pond water every two days, during the months of July and August,

and to listen to them once a week for any special needs.

I agreed to their requests and sat down on the steps to listen. The worms grew quiet when the eldest began speaking. According to her, Thoreau was a constant hummer. He would sit on his door stoop for hours and hum his own compositions. It was one of those original tunes that so impressed her ancestors, they asked if Thoreau would teach them the melody. He had hesitantly obliged as he did not think he was very good at composing.

Because it was 3:00 am, I asked the worms if they needed anything before continuing. They said they had been well fed before leaving Walden, but would like some water, so I poured a little into each container, after which they began to hum one of the most unusual melodies I have ever heard. I was transfixed.

The sound was like the combination of a refrigerator humming, a musical saw, and the lower register of a flute – a combined drone, hard to imagine, and strange to hear. I had never heard worms hum before, but I was captivated by the tune, which they assured me had been faithfully passed down through generations of Walden Worms. I listened to the melody more than the unusual humming. When they finished, they told me I was the first human to hear Thoreau's composition.

The tune imparted images, as many old, good tunes do, of a world where there was harmony; where there was give and take between nature and man, composed at a time when what was essential was exchanged or bartered. It had a a magical quality, conveyed through a simple arrangement of notes. After the worms had finished humming, all I could do was be silent. Nature, after my period of silence, seemed to utter a deep, profound, YES!

The tune was an affirmation of life, so lovely and endearing that, unfortunately, it seemed out of place in today's world. Due to cynicism, brought on by politicians, and too many years of too many wars in the world, my mind almost rejected the idealism and peace it expressed, especially through the innocent humming of those worms. It was written not long after Thoreau and a friend had accidentally set a fire that burned over 300 acres of Walden Woods.

When dawn arrived, I thanked the worms and came into the house, where sunlight was beginning to shine through open windows, to write all of this down.

The worms are living happily in my compost pile. On many evenings, following the night they hummed that tune, I have sat beside the pile, listening to amusing stories, and other tunes, handed down through the ancestors of the worms. Through them, I continue to have a hopeful view of America. It had never seemed possible that worms could be wiser than politicians.

One of their stories involved an ancestor who, after hearing there was a human organization named, "Daughters of the American Revolution," decided she should have the right to address that austere group because her great-grandmother's great-grandmother had received the inside scoop, so to speak, from a participant in the revolution.

This matriarch, after comparing what she heard from several of her friends, upheld the prevailing belief among all worms that Revolutionaries were essentially the same, toes and noses, tongues and cheeks.

About the Author

Louis Sinclair is a poet and artist who began writing poetry early in life. He earned his MFA in Creative Writing from Goddard College. His poetry has been published in magazines and periodicals including: Southern Poetry Review, Maine Times, Ubris, Off the Coast, Kennebec: A Journal of Maine Writing, and Onion River Review. Sinclair's art has been exhibited in museums and galleries such as: The Farnsworth Museum, Bowdoin College Museum of Art, Royal Hibernian Academy, National Gallery of Ireland, Oliver Dowling Gallery, United Arts Club and other galleries in the U.S. and Ireland. Sinclair served in the US Army, Infantry, 1963-'66, including a tour of duty in Korea, where he earned a Black Belt in Taekwondo. *Imbrication* is his first collection of poems.

www.ingramcontent.com/pod-product-compliance
Lightning Source LLC
Chambersburg PA
CBHW061338040426
42444CB00011B/2984